The Dedalus Press

Working for the Government

Gerard Fanning

Working for the Government

Gerard Fanning

1999

DEDALUS

The Dedalus Press
24 The Heath
Cypress Downs
Dublin 6W
Ireland

ISBN 1 901233 38 3 (paper)
ISBN 1 901233 39 1 (bound)

Acknowledgements:
Some of these poems, or versions of them, first appeared in the following journals: *Dlí, The Honest Ulsterman, Krino, Poetry Ireland Review, Responding to Leopardi* (The Dedalus Press), *Soho Square 6* (Bloomsbury), *Toward Harmony* (A Celebration: for Tony O'Malley: Dedalus), *The Whoseday Book.*

Dedalus Press books are represented and distributed in the U.S.A. and Canada by **Dufour Editions Ltd.**, P.O. Box 7, Chester Springs, Pennsylvania 19425 and in the UK by **Central Books**, 99 Wallis Road, London E9 5LN

The Dedalus Press receives financial assistance from An Chomhairle Ealaíon, The Arts Council, Ireland.

Printed in Dublin by Colour Books Ltd

for Bríd

CONTENTS

PREAMBLE

Like a limpet recording its fastidious journeys
I may never know the music of the world
But I can fathom time. This trail begun
Through ten thousand neap tides, sees Amundsen,
A watcher of the pools, trace silver coils
Rounded like ear-lobes listening for the footfalls.

Glimpsed as a prism on the radio telescope,
Hauled like a bow on the raised strings of the bridge,
Was that a change of pace or tone?
A wave or a particle? Or just the ice floes arguing?

I. ALMA AGAIN

JULY IN BETTYSTOWN

When the linen flaps open
With its east coast view of the Mournes,
And Ian Flemming novelettes
Hide in a pile of fragrant clothes,

There is always the sea —
That reeling silence on a line,
And the clay like ground tarragon,
With its stench of burnished brine.

And always the hint of fire,
The thatch in its myriad parts,
And the air full of black-tailed grass
That some times has red hearts.

A CYCLE ON BETTYSTOWN STRAND

The nuns worked at their offices till noon
While on the strand I hummed a cycling tune.
And truth to tell, and on my own,
I rode the arc towards Morningtown.
The nuns meanwhile in squat lean-tos
Dreamt of milk and its residues,
Quiet hearts till the evening sun
They shrieked down to the drifting foam,
In pirouettes childlike and humane
Curious lives in an airy domain,
Where one-piece black bathing suits
Cradled skin in the habit of truth,
Showing how silence goads technique
And heals the profane in a pathetique.

LAYTOWN RACES 1959

While searching for a place to land
My beloved aviator trails his voice
Like a tea stain in the sky.

For he is running dry
Across corrugated chalets, open fenlands
And a prairie of saline fields.

He wonders how far above the tide mark
We should stake out his course
While reeling in a line of stage fright,

And though the radio has no report of this,
I see the shy heat of the dunes,
The beach becoming crowded

And men strolling down Tiernan's Lane.
Why then should my mother say,
In thrall to the turning of the year —

He will come from the marsh road
Past the links and the bawn?
For decked out in khaki

I'll soon be called to eat or swim.
The horses are held back with bunting.
A languorous tide is coming in.

ALMA AGAIN

My father has travelled down for the weekend.
He tip-toes from the scullery, yearning I suppose
For his smoky rooms where men exhale,
Talking of horses, guineas, Redbreast
Or the whiff of shag tobacco in an ox-tail.

His pipe snorts like a little pot stove,
As he sneaks over the sleepers to the far bedroom.
Linen flaps in the rust-embroidered air,
End of July 1951, he comes into his own,
And I almost feel I am there.

Only my mother can say this wasn't true,
Though when she closes her eyes chanting vespers
She reveals my snow-blind tattoo.

MY FATHER RETIRES
LIKE TERRENCE MALICK

Nabokov's French doctor,
The one who said that in near relatives,
The faintest gastric gurgle
Has the same 'voice',
Scares me into the garden
To spray for codlin moth.

Not the bushy headed codlins for goldfinches
Nor the smell of the leaves slightly bruised,
Or the codlin hedge that secures a walk,

But the larva that feeds
On the kernels of apples and pears.
My father taught me when to spray,
Using as an *aide-mémoire*
The drizzle smell of mildew,
And he armed me with a drenching gun
With its dead bouquet
Of Jayes distemper leaking at the brim.

So while the moths laid their eggs
Near the end of June
I would attempt to emulate
His feeble whistle tunes —

That one about the boll-weevil, perhaps,
But more likely
I will be lying down and dreaming,
Of those branchy locusts
Coming with news
Of their own Armageddon
Out of the *Days of Heaven*.

SNOWSTORM

Snow all day, an eiderdown of wet clay
Basking and banking, coming into land —

How many days since we left you
Snug in your little basin underground?

The blank cold as you settled in
Will be an erasure; dusting, muffling

As its echo and bounce
Plumes like a broadcast — *son et lumière* —

In this extraordinary year start.
The few cars that waltz on bolts of lace

Slalom on the kerb's incline
Petitioning trees to embrace —

And I recall how Captain Scott's men
Watched in awe a model of St. Paul's

Float by in the Antarctic.
Such infelicities, such confusions,

As the phone inert in its cradle
Starts to ring. A friend enquires of us,

The living alone and infirm,
'The pubs are still open, shall we adjourn?'

THE FIFTIES PARENT

When he smiled, Khruschev hovered towards me,
Airbrushing days with bliss,

And his bald baby's wrinkled face
Was almost touching, almost miming a kiss.

II. THE QUAKER WALL

THE QUAKER WALL

The stuff from the hedgerow
I thought might be my laurel wreath,
We cut back one evening
Near the end of July.

Honeysuckle, bramble, a nest of freesias,
And copper tubes
That whitened like bamboo,

All of which — muck and scree —
I forked and hauled
And over the Quaker wall I threw.

More like imaginary clay pots,
These uncovered manholes and drains
Are gathered up to lie on these pages
Until they can be rearranged.

DOUBTS NEAR COOSAN

We must have looked like a swimming stag,
head up, eyes in the dark
around Hare Island, around midnight.
We called for the monks in the little interior,
so little we could have made Borgesian copies
to roll like stitched or buttoned canvas
and pocket those lares of worship —
like the smiling garden Buddha, who holds aloft
a waterfont as a source for all the washes.

Though this was just an early morning skite —
the outboard opening its throat
to loft us round like a silly circumnavigation —
there is nothing to worry about.
Record it now, years later, a night out
to drink beer or its time might disappear.
Yet to come so far on a whim
and be caught fast in the breaking moon,
peering into the parallel lives
of our darling co-habitees,
we are so ignorant and arrogant to patronise
the night moves, the domestic shuffle of these.

MURPHY'S HEXAGON REVISITED

i.m. Patrick King

Ten years after our March race across Ireland to Omey,
Volkswagen replaced by a Renault, I visit the hexagon alone.
Through a stumbling graveyard, past a couple saving hay
In this wet summer's one God-given-day.

Fifteen hands high it appears to stand,
Like an old English thrupence weeping bronze into sand.
And though beguiled in its space — a dovetail net of mercy —
The sloped bed, stove and desk covet the margins of sea.

But who owns this washing line, these lazy beds that curl,
The zigzag of hedging as the light bars unfurl?
And is this a right-of-way, did I walk across or drive,
Is this the latitude, the one day the sea does not arrive?

THE BRIDEGROOM IN MOYCULLEN

On the day you were to be married there was a giddy air, and I was asked to take you out, so the guests could stay clear and gather their thoughts. With nothing in mind we drove, turning right for the logical route down off the main road to the lake, visible, shining and discreet, lying back in its thirsty light. But when the road finally gave out and we had come face up to a farmyard where four or five men were loading sheep, or unloading as the case may be, it could have been a backstreet on the lower side as some deal unravelled before our eyes. I had to three-point the car back to the road of tar and through a veil of flies and oaths, we left that morning meeting of souls. The wedding party began in bright sun, unfinished business, work to be done, and the evening passed over unconcerned as though what brought us to these days would be all we retain out of the land we erase.

SILENCE VISIBLE
ON THE LOUGH INAGH ROAD

The few lodges are closed still
and the caretaker winter staff
burn the rubbish that accumulates
in some version of prior time.
Opening windows turn and turn about
they check the paintlines,
while that skitter of antifowling
fondles the tied-up lake boats.
Here, things occur, as if without cause,
or in a dust waltzing as it falls
raised pontoons rake the lazy water,
a plateau of derricks slithers on guys
of steel, while archipelagos of sound,
those cries in slipshod time,
are the stuff of intrigue
yet to be revealed.

NORTH/WEST

Making off for our autumn break
We stumble through the B&Bs of Leitrim and Sligo.
At breakfast there is the shredding fax
Someone's reservations about the weather
Turning to tickertape perhaps.
But these tandem falls
Bring us to the Villa Nova in Drumcliff
Or the Benjamin Franklin in Drumahaire.
And when our car idles
In some grassy *leataobh*
I watch Mr. Kaplin check out
Of the Plaza Hotel in New York
On route to the Sheridan Johnson
In Rapid City, South Dakota.

Such confusions arise
In taking on a job that might become your life,
So if this were crop dusting time
We might be in danger.
But the weather outside is rainy
And the fields are neat
In their black plastic dresses,
As if we had worked all summer
To get to this. So hold out your hand

And lift me onto the forehead of stones
Where pollen speckles our skin,
While in the ghost of a copper rinse
That magnesium smell
Of October rambles in.

ABOUT ABSTRACTION

No more unusual are the salmon smolts.
They flee Killary, sprouting wings,
In a droning helicopter out of their element
Into the weightlessness of things.

MOVING INTO ST. VINCENT'S PARK

In the space that is always new
I check the joists for sleepwalking,
The cornices for collisions,

And the wired abstractions
For the buoyancy of emissions.
Though the keel is battened and spliced,

And the upturned bar
Rocks on its stanchioned coasters,
I wait like a beaded bowl

For that mythical rip tide.
But where are the owners of each silhouette,
Whose dreams and affections are gone,

When in the wonder that still remains
With all the Pole's realignments,
My window faces its same threequarters —

That glinting parabola of light
Like the battery cell of a lost comet,
Swimming far in the zones out there?

DUSK WALKS

We walk the same route every night
Trying to fathom the small debris of cars —
How coils, springs, sprockets and rings
Dither in a tired samba,
Until scuffed along pavements and gutters.
On the West Pier tufts of wild wheat
Spear up in a jaunty confident air —
What do we think we are doing here:
Hopelessly colonizing like these foolish seeds
Or walking off excess and fear?

As the mailboat breathes its drift of sooty snow
A bushel of love on spread arms
Wheels from its flaky undertow,
And dreaming there on plashing lines
Garrulous eyes and shy lights
Wink back seeming to say —
The noise of the world is so terrible
We can endure it only
By being coated with drowse.

SHINGLES

This is a peppercorn deal
With trembling late snags,
A fault line fracture

With insincere blight,
A bubble settling itself
Splayed on the electric field,

A tripswitch that failed to ignite.
As though a surface, all noise
Could be rude with the world

And would inevitably dissipate —
A turlough, a name only,
Lapsing in a thrill of dissonance

While the music of its drone
Chatters away in a shin dance.
So we shiver and demur

As if this rush for a cure
Could entice the dormant plagues
And all their little retinues.

CLARE HOUSE

We are rocking on a frozen bed,
Prow, like a Boyne Coracle
Oars up-ended, held fast,
And we tense our stomachs
To let each other pass.

A barge or yacht might break free,
But we have tons of oak
And underneath the snarl
Of telegraph and telephone.

PAPIER-MÂCHÉ

In school we raised our world
On a script of papier-mâché,
Mountains folded on the legal notes,
Rivers embraced the steady downpour
And winter fields floated off unread.
So my aquatic-veined preliminary maps,
Arbitrary and self-important,
Might just have got it right!

Today the charts of ice and snow
Bleat and punctuate a different lie.
They speak of the occasional music of rain,
The percentages when navigating unmanned
As though my new répétiteur should play
With the morse of the Benny Goodman band.

REHEARSING BECKETT

Beckett walked the East Pier
To plead with Neptune, to entreat —

And McGovern like MacGowran
Now mouths the words
On his cellular, mid-week,
Mid-winter, Hijera.

Is this what it means to be
Anointed, unexamined,
A tattler on the West Pier
Without a thought or a care,
And oblivious of the furies
Roused by the pilot light
Of my solitary Disque Bleu?

APRIL 1963

At the end of December with the sky dark and full
Bud Powell creates the hyphen for Dexter Gordon
In *Willow Weep for Me*. Some encouraging voice
Has its moonlit brocade filtered down
As the session's altimeter prints the air of Paris 1963.

I have forgotten my classroom and Glenn Gould's silent holler,
You could forget everything when days are filled
With notes like these, the tempo of fahrenheit and centigrade,
The composition of oil on frieze, though it might yet snow,
And in the morning the little footprints will be
Quavers surfacing through the undertow.

ART PEPPER REMEMBERS PAUL DESMOND

The way the air shifts you would think
there was no medium out there —

all notes cut from the flame of ice
will cherish the blow by blow, I scare
into the vacuum that is already gone.

And there is no accounting for this,
what we walk and talk in
is essentially humbling and flattering,

though what it all commands
is this somnambulant line
clouding the issue with its beat and its time.

I am riding down through smoke and vapor,
trying to remember not the air itself,
but *this* air, this lithe composure of song —

how the disparate necklace of plucks and beats
could challenge the dissonance of wrong,

how our cell-lights and honeyed filaments
ooze a yellowish fire,
and how I bruise smoky alphabets
as I watch your silhouette retire:

all I want from the plume you exhale
is to fill my lungs over again.

ST STEPHEN'S DAY

After the church service
We park beside the cemetery,
Waiting for the drenched mourners
To pass by.

Leading us in trenchcoats
They resemble the break-up continuity
Of that civil war film,
And we, the peripheral characters,

Smirking in the almost out-of-shot.
Though we may genuflect
And catch the squalls
Trailing their five minute lulls of blue,

We take this chance
To stand and listen
To the bleached white epiphanies
And the little offices,

Where space conceives infinite space,
And breviary translates into missal.
So stand clear
On this St. Stephen's day

At the edge of one version of events,
Where our thinning shadows
Define the hours
Of the pale immaculate sun,

But fails to retrieve
The picnic sites,
From Kinnegad to Kilcock,
The truck stops on Route 66.

LEAVING ST. HELENS

The swarm of black-clad novices
Walking past our door
In groups of three

Vanished overnight.
Now as fields
Fill with rape

And the perfumed garden
Reverts to pasture,
The great house resembles

An impromptu barracks.
A world is being
Mobilised or demobbed,

Doors flung open,
Moon-dazed clocks
Running fast —

And like sappers
Lost in the North Wood
We lean to the right

Listening for our balance
While the earth drags
Beneath our feet.

Time is moving away.
It happens like that.
People lose interest.

THE ERNE WATERS

If Ireland holds with Mercator's cruel web
I think tonight of the Ballinamore canal —
The smart-card hydraulics, a love unto itself.

But should the locks become undone,
That wine-dark cargo, that wonderful weeping chaos,
Might tip like a snagged gutter

On our makeshift pellmet of clip and anchor,
To feed the gravel bins, basins and pots
While we pan for the glittering aurora dust.

SKETCHING STILLBIRTH

The femerell with its louvre
    and string of smoke,
the callows and that fatigue
    they call on.

The pipit's drone,
    the bushes of artichoke,
the windowless dorm
    smelling of eiderdown.

QUINSY

Imagining I had quinsy
I gave the grass a quiff
where it was turning to meadow.

But just as a fever
curls in its own smoke
I found it hard to swallow,

that a guillemot
blown off course
could succumb to rumor,

or eyeing sweet william
in my thatch of garden,
come down on the side of caution.

And I could be his nemesis,
his thorn, his briar,
though I could as well

resemble the red kite
ghosting a saraband
through the Coto Doñana,

as I know my nurse
who tethers the spatula
will tease the cipherings

of bile and sand,
while we search for the kiss,
the signature, the error.

MOUTH MUSIC

It shouldn't come down
to anything so crude
as the stone at Blarney.

But it was you who said
that kissing its runic lines
with legs agape

might lead to talk of farney,
or so I mumbled
as we took the floor,

the band striking up
a salty Cajun score —
and though I have stumbled

through the grace notes
strewn amongst
Brendan Behan's patois,

I trace my craving
back to the slime left
on our plate of rue and blather.

[Note: The Letters of John Cheever (Jonathan Cape) 1989. Page 228. Brendan Behan 'Now that I'm off the sauce I'm much more interested in farney'. 'What is farney' asked Mrs. Vanderlip. 'Farney, mam', said Behan, 'is an abbreviation for farnication'.]

CROP CIRCLES

Optics swam as it pawed and stretched
before coming to, with tiny fists clenched.
Somehow that spirit never stayed clear
when we sent it to London for its little acid bath,
but on the green baize of Crumlin
we idly traced its smooth belly and groin.

Now in a foolish way, as it pines
for a bed of cloves, a den of mulch and carbon
we see it as a rogue sign
to stretch the fields of turpentine,
an impression of tallow in an inky duress
to tuck and pin these shipping lanes,
these freshly dug canals,
like a spinning thurible of excess.

A RED CITY JOURNAL

*

Like an addendum we thought to emerge from geogra-
phy
Into the slim ventricle of Via Dante —
A windbreak or a firebreak, a breather
Before the goldrush of another summer.

*

But further into the addendum, a snow-blind quietens
The swagger of the time-track
And some ethelation gathers force —
Annex, colonnade, or a dream of bones,
As we rince our oil and gel
With the stout bottle of angostura bitters.

*

Lost in the warp and flutter of the portico,
Creeping past that abandonment,
Is a space for the less divine
Who would never confuse an ox-tail
With the beaded stump of a pig's trotter,

But might incline to fecklessness
Or use a tea-stain to establish veneration,
Or think the space that plumes on high
Is tethered to the swing of a metronome.

*

I could now open De Sica's parentheses
And in that studious arbor
Line up time, blow circles,
And prepare to stand outside myself.
But we embrace the armada of semiotic smells,
Studded almond and coriander,
Powders like the silk of perfume
Spread-eagled in their tall bins,
While *The Garden of the Finzi-Continis*,
Its vanished, decaying, melancholy glamour,
Is every closed door
Guarding the parallel calm of absolution.

*

At the Porta Barricana, a pilgrim halt,
A familiar largess becomes a further incidental —
A tree space, a breather, a chapel of ease,

Just as the running track of our tram
On the enamel of the bled stones
Improvises tide-lines as contrails
To mimic the nave of the sky.

*

From the cold of the Apennines
Come rain and its calamities —
Benevolent spring bells, spattering leaky chimes,
The stench of mallow, eucalyptus and pine.

These basketfuls of sodden air are a siphoning
For the finches as we walk down Via Agusto Muri,
And as though in a forest
The sky echo drums on our fontanels.

*

The phone machine takes all the messages,
Outside a yardman burns March leaves,
While the woman overhead
Plays skittles in shoes with high heels.
You lie feverish in your cot —
My mother or my daughter —

And your side table has expectorant, powder tots,
And drugged sleep's burnt magenta.

*

To a pension on Via Drapperia,
Once a two-hour rooming house.

The taxi driver smirks as he gathers our bags.
Surgical room, like post theatre,
Tiled floor, raftered ceiling painted white,
Wardrobe, writing desk, fake chandelier,
An old radiator, quiet —

What are these signatures that cannot be undone?
We guard our language like a foreign tongue.

*

Our last look at Neptune, mocking the photomontage
Of resistance in this red city.
One small postcard print has a man hanging forward,
Dead standing at his shooting post —
His working smock belies a petulant ghost.

Retreating down that silhouette
Of inky grains and dots,
I steer toward the catacombs
Where painted heatpipes yawn and cough.
And groaning like a ship at sea,
Adrift in the balm of a eucharistic night
We empty the bilges in the marine pantry.

SHE SCRATCHES HIS WRIST

She scratches his wrist once or twice
They tell in signals of their private vice.

I am a witness, not some eye from above
Some things we do not know, or only tell in love.

PRINTING THE LEGEND

The train journey into Venice
Pulls across the morning swamp,
Through what one painter might hold
Was turmoil, written into grains and pigments —
Or so our host retold.

In Ford's *The Man Who Shot*
Liberty Valance there is a similar
Black and white chamber
Of dots and smoke
Where a train parts the prairie
Like a mink admiring its coat.

These are false starts, like a false dawn.
But how else could Ford,
Or Fellini in *Amarcord,*
Begin to print the legend
Except to say, the lead story
In today's *Shinbone Star*
Tells of who is the toughest man
South of the picket wire.

HOMAGE TO GEORGE ELLIOT IN NEW HAMSHIRE

Twenty two years or more
and I transplant the twenty-two volume
complete works of George Elliot
up to my little attic store,
which now takes in the panorama
of the Quaker graveyard
none greater than its neighbour.

As we settle in, I recall
how I gathered autumn fruit,
driving through Bethlehem, Medicine Falls,
sober villages on a greyhound's morning suit.
And dreaming of that past,
Elliot on her shelf, I come up for air
in the arms of my own self.

WORKING FOR THE GOVERNMENT

Walking these cut-throat fields
Far from the latest outrage,
My thin-lipped parchments
Show the short, sharp inlets
Where the Atlantic blares.
In the drone and swathe of meetings
We tell how money allocates,
How long corridors
Stretch into the lime of mid-evening
And how chimes rise and bathe
Like a submerged village of commerce
Hanging onto the edge of the world.
Now we have only distance —
Documents on deal tables,
A feathery importance mumbling
Incoherences, as here in Easter Week
I rewrite the cloven, haphazard
Labyrinth of the order of my life.
Hardly the stuff of obituaries!

LENTEN OFFERING

Though we have nothing to show
for all our talk of drizzle, colcannon,
and a glossary of moss,
on St. Patrick's Day in Bologna
we unwrap our 'living shamrock
(ready to wear), conceived near
the monastic settlement of Skellig Rock'.

But it refuses to reveal itself,
or to set sail in its vial of tepid water,
like a mauve lily,
unimpressed to be roused so soon
its belly shows off a spray of liver spots,
confusing seepage with a tang
of cancerous vermouth. Undaunted
I prepare the mock silver paten
and bless the little tangle
as if we were back in our bedroom
all those years ago, saying mass.